LIFE IN THE SINGULAR

SELECTED POEMS: 1993-1999

ESSENTIAL POETS SERIES 126

Guernica Editions Inc. acknowledges the support of
The Canada Council for the Arts.
Guernica Editions Inc. acknowledges the support of
the Ontario Arts Council.
Guernica Editions Inc. acknowledges the Government of Ontario through
the Ontario Media Development Corporation's
Ontario Book Initiative.
Guernica Editions Inc. acknowledges the financial support of
the Government of Canada through the Book Publishing Industry
Development Program (BPIDP).

CLAUDE BEAUSOLEIL

LIFE IN THE SINGULAR

SELECTED POEMS: 1993-1999

TRANSLATED BY DANIEL SLOATE

GUERNICA

TORONTO · BUFFALO · CHICAGO · LANCASTER (U.K.)

2004

Excerpts from *Le déchiffrement du monde* (*Deciphering the World*, 1993),
La manière d'être (*Way of Being,* 1994), *La vie singulière* (*Life in the
Singular,* 1994), *Rue du jour* (*Daystreet,* 1995), and *Exilé* (*Exiles,* 1999),
all published by Les Herbes Rouges.

Antonio D'Alfonso, editor
Guernica Editions Inc.
P.O. Box 117, Station P, Toronto (ON), Canada M5S 2S6
2250 Military Road, Tonawanda, N.Y. 14150-6000 U.S.A.

Distributors:
University of Toronto Press Distribution,
5201 Dufferin Street, Toronto, (ON), Canada M3H 5T8
Gazelle Book Services, White Cross Mills, High Town,
Lancaster LA1 1XS U.K.
Independent Publishers Group,
814 N. Franklin Street, Chicago, Il. 60610 U.S.A.

First edition.
Printed in Canada.

Legal Deposit – First Quarter
National Library of Canada
Library of Congress Catalog Card Number: 2003113946
National Library of Canada Cataloguing in Publication
Beausoleil, Claude, 1948-
Life in the singular : selected poems / Claude Beausoleil ;
Daniel Sloate, translator.
(Essential poets series 126)
ISBN 1-55071-188-1
I. Sloate, Daniel II. Title. III. Series.
PS8553.E29L53 200   C841'.54 C2003-906041-1

CONTENTS

EXILES

Exile I

Your mouth spewed out
black rivers
of poetry

I had moved
too close
words took direct aim
at the burning core of things
those passageways
connected to the unknown

You were living in the mountains

I was seeking the obscure meaning
in other dimensions
the gloom in merriment
that tensions postpone

Elsewhere I think
elsewhere I said
or rather I don't know anymore
what I think or said
what is not said
and yet explodes

When you speak of existence
in my memory
you rise
and mime the space
where beings
slip fleetingly away

I'm learning the dictionary
heady moments as I take dictation
the dry weather disappears

You tell a story
as your gaze
is transfigured

The hours desertify in vain sounds
plough mountains of disorder
no resistance is left
beneath the surges
of a conscience wounded
to find itself to be this lonely being
using words both hard and frank

You know the defence
and the lure of the glimmers
folded rounded
beneath closed screens
whose excess is gone into exile
become familiar

You speak and you repeat
the wild spiral
of the wind and its grandeur
Words rise in flight
write the marvel
of a poem engendered
by necessity
The silence in absence
washes away my grief

Exile II

Banished to the pure aftereffect of loss
while rage
without glee
has spotted us

I rediscover the distances
the images the same
the other
and the panic

You appear
adventurous shadow
hailing the spark
word of air
with wings

The origin of one word
I can hear it clearly
in your wild speech

The exile is merciless
toward those that fear
has left defenceless
before the morning's strain

For a few awakenings now
amidst our turbulent moments
silence has prevailed
sacred
and we've been calculating
what in us is being tested

perfect distance
secret and unmentionable

My friend of the broken pieces
you know wine and flight
the wind rolling its syllables
traces the procedure
of what a gathering of chance events
would be beneath the yoke

I see you moving over
the scars of an island
a project to be
of watchful ecstasy

The unformed is relative
a ghost a shepherd
the starting over
a very old and intricate weave
a ravine of pillaged words
orchards oranges torrents
intuitions spill over
into another country
that a poem unifies

I ask you not to leave
don't leave an exile
I ask again I beg you
I'm not cheating when I say
don't leave an exile

The unknown cuts through the night

Exile III

Autumn kindles its glow again
in the ashes
you the exile
you take on your nobility again

I don't know if pain
if the violent colour
dawns and frenzies
haven't burnt the hope
of a flight to an impossible
elsewhere
strange as the nostalgia
of dreaming of loving
the words of silence
in laughter too loud

Leaving like dreaming
life drives me there

With a gale of years
between rituals
and the breath of the wind
this mutation carries
my regrets
to the gates of heaven

I can see the murky waters
the abysses and the neons
of an imperfect city
to be discovered
broken

No pact
no act
the threshold unpassable
ridiculous
does nothing

Words are useless
in this subterranean prelude
just a horizon cleaving in twain
the flowing manes of the leaves
as they blow and bend
above the river
sonorous as they die

The process of forgetting
came along next
with no explanation
with nothing at all
into the daily void
into errors by fear
free
the word shone bright

We assume a world
lived parallel to ours
where maps only imagine
they show what was silence

Exile of the deep cold
and fires and audacity
I'm asking for peace
peace and nothing but peace

Exile IV

You translate the surprise
of the zones of silence
entering by day
into other solutions

Alone
by ruse you want
to pass through the improbable
repertoire of spectres

For memory we will have
the interplay of the poems of night
and red and festive airs
at evening fallen
opaque

With sighs
with distress
far from the body concealed
in a country with no name
you speak again of those ideas
that concern elevation

All recedes
the white makes fantasies
and the years well up
melancholy divided

Far away
you tell me far away
and yet I draw near

a sole question
is it so ridiculous
to know that love
is lost each day
of writing and thinking
the real is possible

Places are lines of writing
along the curve of our hands
they shake off the lassitude
of other hesitations

You didn't make the effort
of bridges and emergencies
you simply gave in
storms have no tomorrow

I believe the desert uncertain
I don't believe in anything anymore
not in doubt
not in the stars
and not in this crossroads
where our words feigned an understanding

Flight
words create
nothing

Exile V

Time in secret
wafts like a fragrance
along the escarpments
elsewhere

The scenario is already other
diffuse
torn from the errors
of an impenetrable life

You are about to meet up
with your destiny
the wind

A fever and the night
these are the full retreat
of unsatisfied dreams

Alone
you vacillate
gently
down below

You are repeating the wait
probably

I do not turn away
from the fate of things

The value of chance
measures the sequences

assigned by a long journey
as donations
to the day's celebration

Gathering my thoughts needs
more than distance
more than the damp
on a withdrawn voice
a defenceless face

Black
are the avowals the denials and the infinite
black
are the hours the flights from the furies
black
is the wind of another continent
and black too
is my gossamer moan

You have crossed the ocean
for the scent
of this silence

Exile VI

I am the man leaning
on his own withdrawal
silent
other than the snap
of fingers joined

Fever
I know nothing henceforth
not the flight
where the aftermath slips away
or the collusion
serene different

My pain lies in treading on ground
composed of burnt words
of invectives that fear
drives to the whim
of understanding nothing anymore
about these perils
of the evening

An inner force shapes this trifle
implacable

Detach oneself without a word
alone at last

A book a lamp
no other compromises
the sensitive life

Reread a thought
jotted down
at the end of a walk
so as to learn the appetite
to live
the voice imitating
genuine sighs
in human counsel

And there's the wind
helping the rebellious
to forget the callous side
of suffering

Lifting the lands
a shape is fond of
I withdraw one by one
the lights of my identity

Tonight childhood
watches over my dispersion

Exile VII

Keep nothing from the survey
not the outcome nor the measures

Transitory
the voice in relation to others
notifies the wind
to describe the conditions
by which the dream
allows the unknown to occur

Once places came to me
genuine
to disclose the kind of passion
and its cure
slight disorders they were
that ransack everything bereft
of illusions

Solitude invents
a space supporting
the bites and the whims
that between the being and the image
stretch out the words night
and love

From the mountains the shadows
specify the direction
of time and the journey

Before the wounded body
of the day

with no concessions
you have only to set
the summit of silence

Untouchable shape
a sound regulates the movements
of the winding contract
of being

And friend you will be
the voice in the utterable
of a mirage that precedes
your intensity

Exile VIII

I hear that your life
is returning to its origin
this choice I understand
will distance our destinies

I so wish things
would gently flow away
decaying as they go
since nothing is lucid

Whether you forget the books
or I walk in disappointment
in the truth

Truths are inside

All the letters and events
the words hid in delirious nights
the intimate sharings
bogus echoes
I'm burning them
along the lane of this obtuse silence
masquerading as happiness
flowing into norms
that I know nothing of

Seeing the lapses and the fire
aglow in the ashes
the incomplete avowals
the fears
the petty cowardices

the ones I saw and the ones I didn't
seeing all in all its failure

Forget and feel the warm air
of the truth
upon the cheeks of reality
with no more cheating
with nothing at all
forget the details the past
with no illusions
word by word forget
everything
and that's good

Exile IX

There are great plans
in all escapes
things that soar
on vast wings

Flights linked
to passion alone
chance deserts what's known
on high
so as to understand

This voice is not alone
in the wind as it quivers
precarious
listening

Other transformations
along the streets desert
the wild trails
where asleep the dreams may come

Urgent moments are alive
I open my eyes I know
sudden forces
flow through the cycle
and now
have vanished

Elsewhere I could have understood
the absence
the after-void and its release

What is it to fall silent
the wind unravels the question

At the sky's fringes
over there
the birds surround me with courage
and I allow the fragrances of desertion
to wither and wane

Exile X

Life is exactly what it is
solitary
encumbered in its failures
tender and beautiful in its future plans

The cliffs crumble
beneath a sea sky
the few passers-by
move around in the salty air

I withdrew
so I might be in the light

The days pile up I escape
I turn solitary
the history and the person
of my course
arbitrary

The harvest is unfair
I smile at the thought

Preferring wind and horizon
to the closed doors of houses
I repeat things
that inhabit me
that name me
I repeat that freedom
uncovers our destinies

Reality rises
the sea is displaced
I am far away
in osmosis with what guides
the voices of fate

You call to mind
the morals
of disorderly gods

An archipelago
beseeches the sky
to abandon us

Exile XI

Discussions have not
despite this scene
blocked my decision

Leaving is a pure act
I already knew that
I think it would be folly
to ignore
what the heart has woven

Wandering is a gentle flight
a dream
leaving everything again
that will wait for me
opening
upon the steps of doubt
in silence

You watch the city's outline
walking towards it
bearer of a mystery
that seems to be leading you there
To be in the north
white in the memory

Stopping calms the rhythm
restless heart
that other incidents
know nothing of

You trace on the map
the flurried agitations
the streets like a fever
the other stunned setback
of a life

The sole question
set out before you
is that being
sent off on his way

Exile XII

Already the images
are encrusted
without memories

There is infinite desolation
parallel to silence
submerged confined
suffering

Loss though can be heard
loss is repeated in words

The unfinished day
rips away the fog
of morning

Explaining the absurd
can be done through oblivion
inventing for the self
a cascade of lightness

No permission asked
just leave
the other without a dream
the angels grow weary
stopping the holes in boredom

Leave the submissions
the hours
leave
without looking back

now the interdict
has lifted
joyless

Renounce things
ridiculous pacts
organizations
enter with no pretense
into the extreme journey

The other is far behind
elsewhere the day's body
flexes his strength

DECIPHERING THE WORLD

Presence

My language, you the pain
Beneath my words, you fail me
In the day's hazards. Volcanoes
Of ice bear the silence
Of the poems speaking of us.

Language is a childhood to be kept secret.
A vast subterranean region, musky at times,
Raises its memory. The doubting dark
Sweeps away its prophecies.
One must be faithful, the days are helpless.
You tell yourselves this,
When the law insists
On your defending something not really known.

The walls of the mirrors reflect
The void. Time unconquered
Represses destiny's role.
Scattered traces roll on credit
Across the failures in all of us
Well-rooted, to be only what is not.

Absurdly, our folly
Flies haphazard without making
The connection, clad in dead images.
What do remain intact are a presence,
A conscience issuing from the heart's words.

Random

There is a lost voice in the foreign room,
Adrift, no origin other
Than the slyness of a tender wound
Sprung from the terrain's din.

In real movements,
The wall is not present in the groans of the unfulfilled heart,
The face of the abyss lightly touches the indifference
Of the signs of forgotten time.

And that is clarified in the belly of random chance
By the crackling the shadows make.
From the summit of inconsolable days,
You speak of necessities, of supportive tenderness,
Absorbed by the contemplation of human utterances.

Voices

I hear another language being spoken.
Things distance me from its intrinsic beauty.
Is it due to its surface or to the grain of its laws?
It comes close and tells me to keep silent.
Rare, stolen, in the nook of another me,
The origin, the river decimate its legend,
Multiply the voices of the vain torment
Of making everything indistinct,
Without consistency, in the pain
Of some power, of some ignorance still,
Setting ablaze the mystery of distances covered.

Then a spurt of liquid follows, shameful.
This other dimension, mute,
Beyond reason, complete within me
Ever since other humiliations
And so many unspoken servitudes,
Bodies battered by nameless obstacles,
You integrate it into fascination.

A halt overlays the break with irony.
Sounds sing of the street,
Intransitive fresh mixture.
Is it the time for wounds,
The slow agony of dreams,
Or is it the excess of the black sky
Come back from everywhere,
Slack between sounds and voices,
Repeating in absurd duress
That the lamento of your language is ending,
Its cadences adrift beneath the mounds of ice?

Ever since the white moons, the scars
The strain of luminous detours has occurred.
This language has a hundred voices.

Impossible

Across the landscape, a white light
Arrests the exactness of façades
In an endless abnegation.
A window is open. The void
Allows words to whirl in your head.
Grimaces, lowered eyes have screeched
Through so many seasons, so many hazards.

Hanging in the air,
Reality's shapes are suspended from threadbare colours.
In the unfolding of the drama,
You choose moments
To arrest the impossible.

The works of heaven renew the image
Of passers-by pirouetting in this void.
They are the sequel to time invested
In the day to day, in the timetables,
The sufferings, the sadness of the unsaid.
Airy and free they go, restless,
Exhausted, in thrall to a blindness,
When everything has its place, word for word,
Beneath the paths' narrow incline.

Rhythm

The sounds on the screen drive memory away.
Insistent, in the dark of night, it changes course,
Moves greyly forward, molded to cavities that crackle
Across meadows of moon.

Writing remains an insult to levelling.
The sound vanishes. Behind the gates,
Odiferous statues are making signals.
Later, other noises will lighten the rhythm
Of time. Covering over the paths with inner defiance,
Lyricism is visible. Beyond convulsions,
Flee the bright zones.

Are you aware that in absences and reverberations,
An echo foretells the accents of a dream?
The voyage, with a language in distress,
Questions what comes from the garden.
In delicate designs, the rain suggests
It is time to relinquish resignation.

Not This Nor That

The meanders of the back of the hand
Evoke matter and break away.
Keep silent, say nothing,
Not now or ever.
Keep silent still, always,
Smile at incomprehension.

A presence erodes.
The mother of the figures protects the white cloth.
The evening accustoms crises
To sleep next to television sets.

There is neither this nor that.
A frail balance takes upon itself
The surface of sleepless-causing questions,
Arranges strange matters
Whose words in the language support confusion,
As deep as delirium.

Dreaming of its perdition
The immobile heart of things
Groups its sighs in this place.
A pure snow rises from the island
Smitten with a tale of erasure.

Were you in the city near the celestial empire
When the outpourings bore within themselves
The cry of the break,
At the birth of a Sunday?

Homages connect the effects of memory,
In silence culture tabulates sufferings.
Beauty, on the lips of a ritual,
Pushes the research
For a terrain vanished into elsewhere.

Language

In the very detail of a language that escapes me
In the erosion of things, I dare hear this darkness
And all its texture, denialful
The intimate lesion of the other,
When its use surges up from tumult, grooves into edges.

Further on, in the closed abyss,
You understand this suffering,
The door swings shut,
Allows nearly nothing,
Not life or its opposite,
Because invalid the mask lost the words.
These cries, in the beauty with no continuation,
Know nothing of the territory's blackness.

The hours die in denying the bodies
That language has rocked, from the age
Of words, nursery rhymes too wise,
From the rage also, at the awakening of squeals
That skids have left behind upon the ice
Of time. The hours erode, black.

Dispersion

The place integrates the dispersion
Of colours, shades their trajectory
In tattered succession.
Existence is denied, betrayed.
The unbearable sting of silence
Has done its work.

The fever from a perforated culture,
You share its gravity.
From childhood, words in you have been traced
By syllables on fire, tight with pacts of madness.
Fear points its finger
At lacks and irregularities,
Beating time. An insane figure
Shares, between the night and the mornings,
A vileness come to fruition,
Sneaked in among everyone, in the ranks of the unruly,
Shameful, in flight.
The light accents the scenery of the confession.

Light

An immense intuition decays the remade
Life. In the cast of passions
Of the smells of a city,
Childhood reappears.
At the end of an alley, the temporary motif
Of the offense persists, in the light
Of a furious struggle offered up to thought.

A family memory comes down the stairs,
In a way that suits the destiny of everyone,
In a district of humble houses
Like the music from demolished churches.

In the transfer of presences,
Disagreement slips from eyes
When everything is to be created, betrayed,
In tears of rock-hard words.

Hymn and metamorphosis:
One must believe in change,
In the insatiable return
Brimming from mirrors
And stretched by reflections.
Similar to what transforms
Childhood into intention,
The wave exceeds the tremblors
Of the repeated explosion of the ages.
You tighten complicities,
Projecting upon a tableau of the world
The idea of a pillage still more touching
When creatures of flesh, with your words inside them,

Establish exchanges with the past,
That surfaces clutch with a distress
Of bygone days, in accents of the street.

Transparency

Knowing that time devours,
What follows is an energy from within.
The circumstances of a language in tatters
Shake the perfect mouldings,
Powerless, mute.

Anecdotes banalize the drama.
An aerial choice takes place
In cadence with transparency,
Deadly in its viability.

You think you will intervene,
Change the voices,
Offer the most beautiful wanderings
To the snows in mourning,
Family papers scribbled with effusions.
A prism makes a transfer of the inscription
Death had etched
In its flight.

The Real

That hedge holds back the conscience.
The mind imagines the real there.
Glances exceed themselves belatedly.
The other facets of language
Tremble to announce an elsewhere in exchange,
Attributed to the sky's escape.

The unfolding of a singular love
Pounded by tiny squalls,
The precarious flights beneath words.

Time dwells in affection.
Theatre guessed at in a perfect angle,
The esplanade empties.
It is late, in this place,
For eternal life.
The ice carries off silence.
My friends, are you the ones confusing it with night?

Sky

With just the time, you say, of an organic passion.
Oval, a shape glistens. Subjected to speed,
Information shakes up the city
Where you lie in wait, overcome by events,
Repelling whatever obstructs the universe,
Leaving it abandoned at the confines of the fog.

A hand underlines a word,
As the storm dies away.
That obscure presence brings back,
You admit it tonight,
The sounds unmasking
Buried magic.
A love therein resists
Like the way the clouds go.

Scattered, upright,
Prelude to scars,
The hour meditates, sighs.
When words are ripped
One by one from silence,
Their translation derives
From loves and heaven.
How to release these deep abrasions
Sworn not to cry out? Their stories are too short.

The zigzag of lightning perceives the bitterness
Of wordless landscapes,
With no consolation, emaciated, abrupt,
Thoroughbred ever since their origin
Rooted in time long lost.

Each second collapses any enthusiasm,
Dreams and wishes sink, gaps sink,
Forbidden. Under a summitless sky,
The open wound enflames your conversations.

Anguish

Anguish remains. The crossing done,
The voyage centres in the imagination.
Since words change it, the body insists.
The voice, you keep it,
Since without it, outside of it,
There is no language other
Than the closed one of betrayal.

In that living fear,
Everything seems to surge
From a weightless dream.
Words leave the tongue
And reach the flames,
Released now from dreams
Become free of restraint.
For long now, the indivisible
Has raised the path.

The voice breathes you in
Along with that absurd wail,
Folded close along its flanks.
Despite the air spying upon it,
Making its arteries
More restless than talkative,
The memory of mirages
Writes the echo of a tragedy
Above suffering.

Name

An impossible succession,
More often than not of ice,
Conceals the knowledge of things
Beneath chapped wings.
A wound is launched
Into the wind, at every step
That words crystallize
Into a language of endurance,
A little closer to the cold.

You have in your heart
Singular discourses,
It's an intimate way
To talk of this wound
Along which the light
Stretches, essential.
To inherit a name
That random chance transports
Into its labyrinths,
Not much silence floats,
A noise, rather than the void.
A great northern swell of sound
Stark and cold,
Abandons the stranger
Further along, beyond the borders.
The light, oblique,
Detaches itself from repudiated words.

Glance

The glance touches upon similitudes
Between words and the earth
Dense, scattered far and wide.
Meaning resumes the acts of a daily combat,
Sketches strike through the soul, around sudden signs,
Revealing a tension sprung from good appearances,
Saying words without understanding them,
Repeating them over and over,
Always learned from the others,
Without finesse,
Aggressively brandished.

The words of a language
Oppressive, odourless,
Which already for ages,
Here at any rate, no mistake, has imposed itself
Like other languages elsewhere,
Including our own, elsewhere as well.

But here it is a day to love.
The other is unutterable,
Trodden by the solitudes of a language
Unknown by those it erases,
Implacable in its formulas.

All of that points to the north.
The streets catch their breath:
White, hairy, day-dreaming,
Sad, with their frozen edges.
A grating forms the window
Under which words have huddled tightly,

Away from the frost,
Nestled in silence,
For many a dark year,
In the shivers of death,
In the comings and goings, in the tragedies.

The sun is on the wane, a fleeting gesture
Whose arrival you listen to.
If space learns how to live,
Pain can understand doubt.
This distress glimpsed by chance,
In the mouth of another,
Is experienced by distance, essential,
In the ceremony of being.

Architecture

I like to read over this résumé of an era,
Sketching the printed shortcomings.
The map of the streets, I consent to losing it,
My eye on the infinity of architecture.
The tracks, by instinct, lead to a book.
I have to write, thwarting silence.

When the path shrouds itself in a birth,
Will you go towards the word mixed with fate,
With the sport of others in your blood?
Vicious mockery spouted in fits and starts,
Catalogue of wild gestures,
Death's opposite traces the density
Linking invisible sufferings with a grey line.
Waves are a prelude to a dream.
The voice turns into grief, song.
Everything, in this construction, is airy, absurd.
The leaps of the heart are not along the road
Whose maps disperse all anguish.
At the tip of the glance,
The void ices over the unfolding of things.

Grief

There is no law that can crush
The song of a grief
Encrusted in the centre of the mirror.
Only a thaw returns, insoluble,
The image of a disaster. A language
Bruised and renewing,
Attacked in its drift,
Slips away
From fear and sermons,
Submerging words
In the void's absurdity.

An obsession has only the dark
That the light allows it to have.
The language takes words
Like a desire for echoes,
Vaulted in the space made up
Of that light for all.
With no more resistance,
The rivers and their words,
With hasty flow, take off
Far, elsewhere, where you decide between
The dazzlement, the repetition.

Disappearance

Have you torn the letters of the poem?
Words became a language therein
In the complexity of destiny.
Certainly, truth wanted to shine,
But at each bend in the road,
Bitterness was put to rout.

Without pity, without perspective,
It is the intolerable wail
Of the days, with their broken fires,
That reveals the disappearance
Of time to come.
Above the entwinings,
A star, from memory, writes the word winter.
The screens crackle, devious.
At its fingertips, the language
Cogitates the awakening that blows
In gusts across the waves.
In the face of the abetting surfaces,
That link words among themselves,
Everything disappears.

Follow-up

You exhaust the night in a conversation
About what must be done, undone or redone.
Expectancy imagines this absence
Sprung from time and voice,
Like a structuring of versions
Arrived at their peak
Rather than in their ascent.

At night there are plateaux
Opening the pure horizon
To thoughts that crack,
Wild with adventure.
The present listens to words
That language disperses.
With no attention paid to a trail,
Phrases swamp the clock,
As they decode the curves.
Reality, attentive to the deadline,
Places where events take place
Requests a follow-up:
A simple word, addressed to the grey skies.

Risk

The unexpected approach of wings, in the midst of risk,
Recalls in the late daylight
The magic parade of shadows
And a place to sleep
In a little death:
The unspeakable defeat
Of not being. With no mask,
Rejected, humiliated, kicked, tritely
Covered in insults screamed from on high,
A destiny's heart falters.

The weapon is a word of steel.
Clouds revive the frost.
A remark by the wind freezes
The impression the same wind blows away.
The building is opaque.
Fear, blackened, embeds itself in the void.
Walls rise.
Standing there, age crumbles
Without knowing the word loss,
Ignoring the insults
That have branded the others,
The unknown who roam
Amidst the shadows of silence.

Those starving for freedom
Who will never be,
Who have never been,
Which the day grows aware of
In the midst of pained weariness
And will describe their illusion.

Calculate the breakdown
Of groundless rumours,
For the malaise of saying what brings us down,
So late, so late, beyond echoes,
Far from sleep, in the question
At the centre of this obsessive issue:
Can one come alive again
In a language humiliated?

Understanding

Ruins glow,
Huddled in fraternal embrace,
The other evenings of silence.
A slow melody, come from books,
A dream roams beneath words like curtains,
Further on, in a time to come.

There is nothing to understand
But this sudden warmth,
And that the heart opens
To permissable words.
Sunday's speech,
Exposed too much to the sun
And whose games foreshadow
That the word memory
Wears white clothes,
Illuminates the voice at times
Of noisy alleys.

You also, you try
To smile instinctively.
The weightiest knowledge
Is silence.

Oblivion

Nothing is to be regretted. Love words,
Language, in thrall to the wind,
That knows the effects of collective forgetting.
This language promotes a way of speaking
A rhythm among people.
It diffuses a project
In the core of time passing.

Language is a destiny,
Our history, fragmented and transitory,
With its permanent things mute.
It takes you in its arms,
To recount the effort and the desires,
The revolts from dawn onwards, the austere
Night that comes, in the throat
Where the storms of living intertwine.

Amnesia, immobile, opens crises within you.
Visions rise against oblivion.
Winter writes white upon the song's emotion.

Emotion

From the shores of language,
Blind shapes elude,
For a moment, the deluge of sounds.
All returns and all shatters.
Sunk under the weight, changes,
Passions retreat cancelled.

The angels turn scarlet, human,
Their intuitions are ample.
Silence is jostled
In its shelter of laws.
You transcribe these events
As fury shapes them,
Without cutting out the emotion
Nor criticizing the fever
The time alone announces.

Bruises with no day,
That the others understand
As a wounded esthetic
And whose memory is in exile,
Silence the suspicions
Encaged in scruples.

In the direction of fear
That transforms all things,
A tattered stretcher
Folds under the winged bodies
That the wilful light contorts.

Succession

Words have no time and the language rages
Against gathering problems. In a darkening garden,
A line of sleep brings things back to tranquillity.

The translucid time of a difficult language
Finds its words again.
Compassion diffuses what it is you feel.
Causes or follies, and hours
Are dead weights. The precise intuitions
Of the world escape through the pores of reality
Become something else, something even more diaphanous.

So many words beneath silence
Will not therefore have been enough
To tolerate pain,
To return it to its beauty.
Buried under snow and the bodies
Of an alienated attrition,
The language roams, like a prayer in mourning,
Losses overflowing from its hands,
Beyond all hope.

From the succession of events,
Restlessness emerges, slowly settles.
About what comes next,
Violent thoughtlessness,
Everything that hinders
The luminous arrival of necessity.

Paris-Montréal, 1986-1993

THE WAY OF BEING

In this fragment, in this scrap, in this fragment of a fragment there lies nevertheless a hint of a breathless desire to express oneself in a rapid flight that is constant and seldom heard.

Sigurdur Palsson,
Heat Ablaze

There are things
several things
we understand only afterwards
a cold voice
a slow step
in the evening
the last one

A certainty surfaces
the memory of a love
comes undone
the image is truth
I had not grasped it

Mourning and the wind
from a forgotten time
came into me
at the appointed time
I think

Silence invents the night
reconstructs it
alone at the fringe of a landscape
that we hold on to above all
the only light close to us

A vision of time
fades from the clear sky
events transform exchanges
thereupon words become traces of being
an effect of vertigo
upon the body of life

Spell of night
torn from the sounds
of that childhood memory
irregular
I manage to imagine the dawn
in its grey direction
so much does the noise of the day
draw me out of my horror
of not understanding
but also of accepting
because I don't know everything
about what overcomes me
not the far-off grief
or the inner song
in these processes
time is intangible

Ravaged by silence
despite all the tires squealing
on the wet road
in this passage to the day
I imagine a peace
mingling with the incessant
movement
the piecing together of realities
absolute bedlam
unruly and clear
cuts through the night
built of illusions

I don't dream by day
I carry it with me externally
shot through with its crises

and if it happens
that I can forget the racket
it's because I've found
the balm of night

With one hand the day
balances things
that yet tend to flee
into zones of absurdity
where what comes after tries its best
with no mystery

The words of my poem
are the song of a memory
that knows its way
the one I am today
a being dazzled
by violent light

I don't have to decide
the day does it for me
and name the infinite
I cannot do
words disperse
I attempt to construct
something that gives meaning
to tenuous ties and to life
that the simple evocation
of the poem lifts on high

Poetry called essential
originally
I listen to a poem

it makes the difference
and the connection
I listen

Writing like the city
destabilizes the meaning of things
I glimpse places
organized worked out
operating direct leaps
into real life
words weave the rhythm

I am not the actor
of ephemeral drives
that on the greyest day
give a glimpse of what will follow
from what is in me
origin and passion

Ideas for poems
born in a street one evening
dreaming
write the truth
play the game
be the one who writes
what is necessary to live
from singular to essential

I write
I think
of what is deep in my heart
poetry documents my life
weaves reality

into the enigma's wing

I don't argue anymore
about the skies already grey
the travellers in me
have sated their hunger
for no reason I move
the lines that assert
that try to unify
harmony and time
if I speak for no reason
it is not without thought
because to act in this world
means to be confident
that the majority
dwells in happiness
through human ruses
this is not horror
it is simply the position
of a word that weighs
its way of existing
in the silence of the other
yet so near still
since what is written has said so
since the song traces
the only true and wind-pressed
voice of the path
and what this wind writes
upon the table between us
I know is ephemeral
another version of time

In the dim description
of buried songs
I wander devoid of any destiny
in thrall to the white dawns
of the morning
not daring anymore to hold back
the words that from deep hollows
take flight again

I share the absolute scorn
the heart allows itself
under the hand under the science
that another secret departure
rendered rash
while the angel waits
for its fall to the bottom
of a magic pitted
as obstacle against the so delicate
passion of the body
recognized in the morning
ruins mirrors silences
so many plurals dictate
the tragedy the only
outcome of the drama

If I should write these words
in closed periods of time
it would be to find out
after time has passed
whether the most reversible
of the lines of the image
had in its shadow
the decency of destiny

This time I am speaking
not keeping track anymore of anything
neither chances nor waters
the occult pleasures
the furies of the past
under the hand advancing
abandoned to the place
where everything gently unfolds

The poem of space
takes on the explicit shape
prescribed by its vows
to exist in the wake
the mark and mask of a profile
in praise of a common destiny
on city squares
in me everything is reborn
the statues the paths
of this invisible park
where I went to write
the poems of the wind
fecund architecture
with its pernicious perils

What word
become other
displaced by the very light
of the past in the sparring
secret more reviled
than the real abandon
that of the ingestion
of the likely arrival
of ageless solitude

the connector from body to body
when language covers
the surface of things
with crumpled snow
shared and rebellious
more diaphanous still
than the sky's stare

I venture stealthily
around rebellious curves
exposed by the detail
of a glimpsed fresco
glazed and reproduced
on a model
whose order of no return
announces the adjustment
to circumstances clinging to doubt
the givens of the cycle
everything I expend
at a loss along the shores

When I learn
where springs the night
I can do nothing but try
to understand the wheels and cogs
of oblivion's machinery

For a different poem
I've chosen a different ink
without really bothering
about the one that sang
in my hand on that day
when the light was born

from a translucid surface
whose dream dimension
was all I had perceived

Everything goes without saying
where words are concerned
then I think
of the days of love
it's from the poem
that courage springs

The revolt of the stars
that image so close
of climbing towards the summit
denied
other
I accompany it
despite the obstacles
to be imagined
telling what transforms
here into elsewhere
the impossible truce
will say the opposite
the destiny of the poem
is for us both to find each other again

In homage to the city
I tore up pages
more vast than time
its regular sighs
wander through the red streets
of a betrayed hope
I don't know anymore

if I knew the city
or if it gave me
the fleeting illusion
of having on this voyage
loved what was

Solid reality
observes the drift
of sounds that know
how to conceal choices made

Words in diverse patches
assemble
what chance
has held but an instant
engendered
weary of saying
that all is stratagem
the day is endless and flees

A gentleness stirs within me
thinking that the day dies
or that I've forgotten life
and its ringing laughter
holding out armfuls of wild songs
with internal limits
an intrusion speaks of reason
louder than its voice
its only solitude
appointed being or a version
of an infinite shipwreck
with glistening alarms
upon the fleeting eyes

that I saw again too soon
in the night gathering
precarious energy
that I embrace

The most infinitesimal impression of being
sums up the song's density

I imagine the gravity
of the sole beat
that resonates in analogies
surpassing the age lines
of shapes preceded
by the habitual mirror
or still buried
light is depth

I name the storm
of other effects targeted
in daily sounds
the ephemeral city
sums up all these things

Fastened to my lips
are the words glimpsed
around love's passion
upon the image of rain
wisps of fog are frozen
having no tomorrow and no knowledge
it has burst open the sky
of my crippled language

So long as the poem
at a word unjustly
frozen in its flight
by sudden misgivings
is the other and the afterwards
in the enjoyment of the instant
all will be real

One unsuitable thought
yields from the noisy day
the link it has invented
the precise inversion
is light
silence also
in the invariable maze

The arrival of faces
with the appearance
of incredible labyrinths
like thoughts linked
to the sole opening
upon the steps of an angel
caught at its game
I think
since any feasible flight
is an acknowledged body
not far from nonchalance
one's private life
in secret orders
summons the midnight

There is a writing
and right beside the beauty

of a gesture striving
to underline life
its presence echoes
in the voice rattling them
the adventurers
of the advancing day

Just pack up and leave
all alone

Words break the final
concession granted by the mirages
whose restless sounds defy
the tempestuous art of drunkenness

There is no lamp
to sober the mouth
fingers tangled with love
hold the ancient division
of styles and works
conceived in the fullness
of the morning
I know the very nature
of repetition
impedes any action
in these pristine reaches
where the walkers are sleeping

The page is white
its milky body
is not soiled
after being used
it will be something else

without negating its intention
to continue its existence

I took the book
in the slanting light
on the paper words
indicated a refinement
of expression
the impression of keeping
the deepest of secrets
compelled me to change the word
that I intended to write

A frail equilibrium
carries the magic
far into the piercing of place
it reshapes the transparency
of energy

I write of the grey day
the passion of loving
welled up from the beauty
of things and efforts
fashioned for other songs

The scene halts
along another way
the partition of the body
into restlessness
remains the aerial surface
of time's investigations

About the other change
and the night
in luminous substance
words will not speak
in the ignorance of the shadows
the rite carries them
typographically
to the crossroads invented
by the language of an era

Discovery would be the story
of a concrete passion
revealed to the dawn
opening on the song
at the day's fringe
and its repetition

A grey cast overcomes
the whole exterior of things
I know it
from having dwelt in it
at the interior of my days

It is difficult
to imagine yesterday
its weight is reality
once it has gone

I would like to live through
the passive folly
that transfixes that seals all
and walk towards a sky
and its dense sonorities

Writing remains
haphazard
in its arrival

A tale of origins
within me is this universal
book I am contemplating
in love with the night
its explosion scattered
to the four corners
of the intolerable

To be the construction
the pressure to write
by the light of day
within memory's instability

I open poetry
to the wanderings
and to the ships
errors in the collapse
dream up the snare
of unreal disorders

Faint fragrance the hours have
my look out the windows
the other beings
inside me go drifting
their voices fold
melting into time

Reflecting on the way
and its white desire

which life imparts to the book
unfolded across the total reaches
within me outside of meaning
envious of certitudes

It would be a loss indeed
the rain fleeing the aura
of the most immense of visions
that of havens
tempests or choices

The situation between the facts
deflects voice and surface
into a blackened notebook
wisdom blows with the wind
peaceful irresolute
singing of the moment
with its tender opposition

To assimilate the joy
of the body in movement
the evidence from dreams at work

The need to speak
in the total silence
has transferred its passion
to make possible
the confrontation
between cycles of fog

Alone I listen
to the pure reading
to the rare and beautiful sound

of the written material
of body to heart
creating eternity

Morning offered
without a grave
the bodies on the boulevard
rivaling one another in emptiness
ghosts or life
with a semblance of day
swaddled in the grey
of a trajectory and its trappings

From the poem his body speaks
his eyes close to his voice
with oblivion to the other
the other in a fury
of words

Gently poetry
has lost its mistrust
cloaking words in fire
it will speak of its presence
open to strangers

LIFE IN THE SINGULAR

Elegy to the Silence of Loving

I am writing an elegy to the gentleness of living
when the words of the street
well up like a poem
learned by heart
at times

If I enter into dead fragrances
whose memory is in me daily
to wander here and there
from one spot to the other
with no knowledge
borne along by steps by sounds
trapped in the image of a stone angel
when the wind of the streets
comes and breathes at my neck
the bleak and raging words
of infinite suffering

That day I took back my worries upon myself
and I proceeded with no constraints
toward that which already exists
because the hour is crumbling
and everything is about
to become the time
whose visage we immobilize
once and for all

Through the windowpanes
I listen to the books
a fresh breeze cleaves the shadows
at a specific address

I do not feel constrained
I prefer to eliminate
the works of the present
pursued like a dream
by a passing hand
taken with the idea that purity remains
a state of being
foreshadowing the poem
at the cutting edge
of pens and screens
derived from no known model

If the thing is strange
and has invaded my being
it's because it is the stagnant pool
of other uncertainties

And despite this havoc
this sound full of rare air
I learn if the hour has aged
from seeking through the streets
the final consequence
of the secret breathing
inside books glimpsed
along the sidewalks of illusion
speaking of the city and eternity

And I who am still changing
as I lay down my knives
faced with the end of a story
I inundate with everyday words
the feelings of a day
toward another dark voice

who takes the same version
of this way of greeting
that is offered to anybody at all
to be accurate and precise
in the midst of feelings

If that is written
I will take it at face value
believing in the hymns and the sequences
of the means to name
that anguish so scarlet
at the turn of a year
of which nothing remains
at midnight for anyone
because leaving the place far behind
where the body takes flight
is the only quest
open to melancholy

Love has paths
that cloak our efforts
I know I will meet there
absence and totality
giving to the day that passes
its singular fever

This poem is being written
in an upper room
that has become the last refuge
of a bleak January

Empty and earnest
I devour books there

the threshold of words
cuts through the night
it is here on the sill
of a very ancient city
whose sounds cannot erase
what a river contains
of encrusted lines
fluid and more vague
than the fake décor
of the night's open doors
and the metal glint in eyes
speeding in the dark
that no image can reproduce
except in fragments

I am writing this elegy
before the shadows awake
with their members closed
so as to restrain words
describing the vast feelings
of a city revealing
its time and its lights
to the one in his frenzy
and who abandons himself
as he denies
that what he has come to pillage
from the arteries' rituals
is precisely this rhythm
beating with the impossible

Standing near the summit
of the line of Icarus
whose name goes before me

where the hot winds blow
from cycles of light
there are cars
I can see that I hate
and the easy framework
whence all flights are betrayed

Upon this nocturnal way
with its clandestine wings
the hours come to an end still
amazed to have lasted
but abandonment threatens
that which is absolute
consequences will burn
the highest tensions
undone in total silence
they fall and fall
like the voluptuous things
described by him
who has lost his youth

One must learn everything
and cast everything aside
shapes from the past
that often haunt us
with their presence
that propose solutions
we hesitate to let go of

The poet is an expert
in impossible losses
which is why he entertains
the shapes that persist

and with the same impulse
he wants to erase them
and with the same impulse
he retains their essence
as though the past
sovereign and voracious
had a view more just
upon the present

It's at dusk
that the poem worries me
asking me whether the time
has come to bury
in the secret of the night
that which is implacable
and which the silly daylight
was not able to accomplish

And if the angle of a wall
is slanted and streaked with mist
it's because the time at last
has come to whisper with a sigh
beneath those deadly lamps
of expressive quests

It is the black West
that suddenly arrives in these places
with real time at its disposal
along with the soul of things

And tempted by the plenty
I have not given up
binding together opposites

in the heady words
recognized in passing
beneath this indirect lamp light
that gathers up the effect
of these scattered moans
like a livid disease
wandering within
the images in a row
since the evening repeats
the song of an absent voice
and the body of the beloved
is nothing more
than grief overrun with brambles
with thorns of fog
prowling in a room
with its low and secret bed
and no extraction from it
can ever put a stop
to what I imagine to be
the history of my memory

Angel of an unravelled night
with its smells of a wild moment
I will be able to hold on
to your darkest designs
that work between us both
at stirring the imagination

There is sadness
in the word beauty
and evasion still persists
in the word harmony

Therein I can hear debris
of a time pitted
with thefts and shocks
that I cannot verify
whether existence once jelled
for the body is that which
survives only in the dream
of some voracious energy
sweeping away images
toward a more secret place
than the wings of an angel
who has reached the summit
of his nocturnal spectrum

And there in the uses
of a body abandoned
there is a voice
that an echo feels

In the midst of the fragility
of the shadows gathered in this place
I would not have cried out
that the hours pass too slowly
for if the time happens to me
I can only dream
of those strong drifts
like the passion of loving
that is already gone
and has always been
that which is on the wing
and which flies back again

For the fragrance of the shadows
rises from the thin fingers
that know the path
singing of the mystery attained
by the most diffracted of sciences

An elegy plunges me
into dreams of what is to come
and it is a presence
more real than the body
in the core of the heart
dictating these words to me
that have become the sole trace
of so many tremblors

So I am writing about this loss
that having become light
transforms the vision
into a prism irradiating
the whole night long
more opaque than oblivion

I am listening to the lamentation
of a voice nearly hoarse
from the insane desire to have
betrayed with no choice possible
a force so somber
that it would have buried
both the dreams and the bodies
come there to quench their thirst

In the rapture
of far-off tedium

I continue on my way
that is shared by no one
I go forward through the dark
torment of having loved

And yet in the evening
when the glistening streets
impart to my footsteps
a singular lightness
I can still see like a mist
still protecting me
that infinite love
my dreams have created
filled with absolute images
and eternal understanding

And never in oblivion
and never in rage
will the idea be scuttled
that I had discovered
a tender place and wild
that watched over my life
and imparted to fate
grey waves and variables
breaking
over days and nights

The elegy I am writing
is not intended for remembering
nor forgetting either
the effect of a voice
of that body taking on
all the energy present

in the exchange of earth and being
propelling with a rite
out-of-time
in a reversed present
that displaced the banality
of life's different things
restoring its majesty
to the skin's fragrance
a knowing smile
a winged allusion
taken from the stone angel
who at the park's extremity
stands in silhouette
in the snowy fog
wherein I walk far from everything
so close to pain
seeking and finding once more
the illusion of being loved

What is life all about
here upon these shores of time
where memory is respectful
of the slightest feeling
become sand and loss
and mirage and object
of an absence so bleak
the day no longer lingers there

If before my eyes there arises
the image of a departure
I realize once again
that time goes before me

I have lived because I loved
and yet I know
that in a low-ceilinged room
where tears have dried upon the sheets
those moments remain

I will not go back there
but I recognize them
as they speak of solitude
and from solitude dramas high and precious
take flight
with time's dark sermons
interlaced with images
at the breaking points of silence
and whose centre holds
a way of dreaming
of a voice I hear
that has restructured itself
in my deepest self
another landscape
and this one is inviolate
and close to the real

Both chimera and ecstasy
like a guide
that voice inside me
an infinite presence

And it is an elegy
of timeless forms
that from song to respect
hopes in the gentleness of evening
to be granted the pardon

of the angel with his stone eyes
who has ransacked my life
and set it ablaze
in a park bristling
with the feel of mystery

For what can one say about the night
when the hour has forced us
to return to a room
where the memory
of a body resides
the offering of a totality

Poems are still able
to contain these places
to perform sufferings
the intact metamorphosis
in this they bow down
their faces of blackest ink
to give pulsation
to a life reborn

For the life of a poem
is a forgotten body
holding in its hands
the warmth of a lover's breath

A gentleness of living
can become an elegy
to a tone of voice
to a ghost
or to a detail
reconstructing the sequence

whereby the words will gather in silence
of a story
that was meant to be

And I walk toward the streets
toward the others and the dream
the indiscreet light
of a lighthouse wherein the angel sinks
gives meaning to the moment
about which I never know
if it is going
if it is coming
an aura both precocious and closed
of an adventure that lasts
often until dawn
and withdraws
from the truth of a life
which a tempest has changed
the innocence of loving
of believing in the absolute
of abandoning everything to it
in the desire of laughter
at the edges of silence
of a mouth made soft
by the light of dawn
and its melody
telling of the abrasions
on the sill of the grey house
a park dies a hostage
of that first departure
toward other perils

The heart begins once more
to focus on the real
in scenes where the wind
blows its consequences
once again things breech
an opening in the sky
that I can see can imagine
can feel

And I move forward nostalgia free
into the territory of the day
bearing in my head
the shadows of a love
that had given me life
and the courage to be
destroyed and recognized
in the exile of the body

In feverish thrall
an island on the horizon
from these glacial desires
destiny plots its designs

I find myself alone
amidst the extremities of silence
outside of that love
inside it for all time
when time hurries me
to write down the avenues
of a dawn where the softer breeze
of a park open and damp
takes for itself the time to love

And I go with no regrets
the possibility of existing
draws me to the window
touches my hand and the objects
in the entire room
have lifted their shadows

I will never forget
and this is a comfort to me
to know that love
has no limits

The division between day and night
between the street's unruly sounds
and the park's slippery moods
fashions the passage
of an assumed loss
where I find the other
dazed within me
and I grant to fate
the power of the moment

The day is bright
after endless rages
it shows a glimpse
of a way to attain the energy
in time's course
linked to circumstances

For if the sound of suffering
accompanies my voice
if the path persists
upon which I walk alone

it is because I have abandoned myself
to the secret of the real

This is where the wound
can become poem
taking on at the end of the night
the form of an elegy

The joy is infinite
in dictating these words to myself
torn one at a time
from absence with its bleeding wing
folded
free

DAYSTREET

Is it a voice from the parade of things I do not know
How to listen to it or to recognize it has come too late
To tell what has fastened me to the core of a sought-for look
How to reckon how much doubt of the day is lost
Drowned in the debris of the angel of the ruins
In this library there is nothing but shadows
Not long ago the real stopped its pretence at existence
Dreams fade slowly beneath the stones and life
Is speeding away despite the grey calling them back
There is nothing among the voices but the insatiable
        sequence
Of some high tension lost in the rubble
Of the irreparable gesture of having discredited
The hidden meaning in these rites vibrating in the wind
Of instruments whose very presence indicates
That in this place once there were reasons for hope

The song now he is gone coaxes the dead day
To wander among the stones those mute dwellings
Whose cascading light confirms the silence
Unsubdued beneath the legacy of these ruins fading
With the dry blood of misunderstood and sullied tears
There is a distance in this solitude close
To beauty because of the sky filled with dignity's hour
When music becomes once more the gift of meaning
Of existence and being through the movements
That the image embellishes but does not deny its horror
All this carnage of the place even knowledge the air
Without arrogance lost and weightless beyond words
Fallen to dust the shelves lost with their works
Filled with the reasons for dreaming and building
And for loving all human passion even the errors

The amnesias the bodies torn to pieces dead children
Without any study or smile play war games for the tv
The vision of a world a few inches still from the limit's edge
For what is sketched here is the state of beauty as
Sadness unfolds its indecent seductions
To die from that pain without knowing beyond all doubt
The debris is in everyone a failure in everyone
An impertinence of the century responsible for so many
    deaths
This century of progress this century with its mechanical
    angels
Has seen the parade of suffering the other life and the worst
In this kind of stage setting steeped in the intolerable
The only certainty lies buried in ruins destroyed
Backed by the follies of history with its muffled conflicts
Its racisms its silences holding sway in all places
Vertigos unable to deliver into being the other version

The desire to live flows among the broken pillars
There was once poetry science and a geography
The walls proclaimed honour to research and the pursuit
Of a loftier understanding of a vista outlined
In the scorched pages of mutilated books
Now the scene is a photograph
Glimpsed unexpectedly in a gallery on Daystreet
In Paris during a winter when all is tender and grey
When beauty erases the enigma of pain
Howling upon the white table of this gallery
I came back to see the photo that moves me
I feel its sharp presence folded endlessly in my fears
Contemplating the horror describing the madness to me
With no comments to make on laws soldiers or the innocent
Naming no names wreaking no vengence in its utter fragility

The walls have vanished the books are ghosts
In this library opened to the cruelty of the wind
An angel mimes mankind music attempts
To swathe suffering in a slow dirge
Obsession of constructing obsession of surviving
Decisions are made here based on connections to the sky
Exposed to the worst torments it keeps its grandeur
Overlooking neither the past nor the heinous present
Nor the lines of pain that men have signed
Beyond stupidity and the vile cowardice of the narrow mind
Words like images can attempt the impossible
To restore dignity to one's being despite the other side
The voracious horrible poisoner of objective debris
That proceeds in all hate to give form to the frenzied reasons
In which man finds sufficient cause for killing

There are no tables left no children no readers
Except a frail angel with features grey as life
And a ritual music attempting even in peril
To record the upheavals of a pale soul
That could flow through the ravages and give
Love courage to these endless tears to those
Who once have lived and read these things in a remote city
Devastation and concrete a city buried
Under torrents of fire and stones of evil
Whose forces remain a smothered secret
A voice proclaims that the scene is intolerable
That the irrational could still destroy lives
Other signs their severity strewn with beauty
Angels as innocent as the tragic fate of children
Prisoners without a language at the heart of the inhuman
    drama
In this library akin to the purest of visions

The hope of art and beauty and their steady gaze
Insisting among chaos on naming its inverse
And on opening the eyes to the transience of things
And that the slow quiver of violins is dispersed
When a voice rises from the debris seen
In this photo depicting a library
Razed in rage to smutty rubble
With no respect for the body or mind or the spirit
In these thousands of books full of human ecstasy
The library and the angel in the faces of the wind
Pose for a new and fixed eternity
No request now no goal beyond the photo
For the fate of the word hope is hidden in books
Whenever deadly and senseless arms come to blind it

The only thing to know is what is impossible to utter
A kind of misery clinging to the body
Of this library where a childlike angel
Tries its best to exorcise the pain of the wild wind
Destroying time and killing the picture of the city
This image orders me to understand the absurd
Meanderings of language plotting a plan that rises
Toward collective death in the silence of the hours
Conflict of absolute hatred beneath helmeted arms
Beneath the veils of dwellings become targets
Are there any guilty ones I cannot say
This is not what has weight in this strange scene
Is the silence a past brewing to be detected
What is left of comprehension along the ransacked ramparts
All I can see is the grey of relentless pain

There are instruments without any score
The disease of death suspended in the air

Absences make over long-awaited joy
That understood losses can never revive
In this wasteland with its disarmed accents
I am not guilty or rather I am
All is absurd and all answers are empty
There is no room left in me where I could shudder
The worst is on trial in this photograph
Well-defined genesis at the core of peril
My mind's eye rivets this photo glimpsed by chance
On two occasions I believe in an art gallery
Its white walls shimmering with neon
And this photograph with accurate aim
Lays down the stigmata of present pain

Giving minimal information to anyone who sees
Maybe also the meaning of art amidst folly
Of being a balm in the appeasement of the day
And its muffled deployment of the fissures of war
With its cruel image closing the display
Is it by chance that I came across the image
Of a subject I cannot straight off appropriate as mine
I am far away and in my remoteness the body
Turns to folly turns toward the open sea
Desires only to know what is too hateful
Beyond this photo there is a reality different in
Its chaos its ugliness harshness tumultuous and rotten
He who in the presence of a child-angel
Found in a twinkling once again the wings of mystery
He waits an observer stalking foaming waves of rage

In the light rain I came back to the gallery
All was white with silent men holding
Canvases they were hanging no word spoken

The dazzling friezes of a different day
And I searched in vain for the photo
I asked them for nothing they were very busy
Already preparing other selections other images
I went walking in the rain thinking of the angel
Whom I asked to finish my poem
Can you angel will you angel
So much energy needed to alleviate the grisaille
To enhance in silence the illuminated chants
From within one's gaze when density weighs
At the same moment upon a place in memory
Where ruined books give birth to light

Is that what I saw and is already no more
Vanished from a city with its passing passions
In a city that performs its relentless pluralisms
Taking nothing from craters but their constant movement
I remember the image it is engraved in me
Angel listen to my poem if it can soothe your pain
He will start your rhymes over for you and scan them
In a foreign tongue he cannot speak
He will attempt a fresh start at describing his confusion
Faced with that vision torn from the precipice
In mourning after inspecting the grey-streaked strata
Starting by degrees to vibrate with the intolerable
In the precise distance from lethal discoveries
I think I can grasp what is already turning to silence
What is already taking flight among the vanished books

Voices of children of mothers fathers friends
Encircle the improvised fires in these havens
The exposed solitudes of a ruined world are born
That nothing left now can hold back its hopes or faith

For in these dark places music is betrayed
On the sill of the library the air stops shaken
By the void inherent in the unutterable loss
Of a metamorphosis the angel seems to bear
Believing in it is much better than not weeping for it
Through stained glass broken into dried blood splinters
I never speak of these too grave things
Their fate is in tatters their image a suffering
An experience pushes me that is even more opaque
More despairing in its craggy beauty
That I cannot give a name to
So fast does time snatch them away

Is it perhaps the voice of the angel or the books
The child who rests his gaze upon the void
Of this sprawling place that cannot be concealed
This story of destruction and heinous slaughter
Dividing into battles the basic desire to exist
I do not know is it the very idea of the library
Its pitiful display that asks me a question
Can poetry do something in the midst of horror
Can poetry alleviate suffering
Gather it into its words and say I love you
The angel is in the photo and whispers to me to write
That libraries are bodies revived
And that one must lucidly be on the side giving life
With downward gaze and sound of peace as one's lot
Just by itself this simple thought is an action

Can a photograph save an angel
Even a child-angel who plays a hieratical game
Among the bombed debris of carnivorous scenery
Showing respect neither for man nor the era of language

Whose ruined walls preserved its echo
Prepared to transform life giving to each day
Its equal its night so the silence necessary
For each of us is at peace and clinging to the fringes
Of the unknown where the shelves stacked with books
Will invent new steps with faces beckoning
Is it this library's voice or the murmur
Of the angel is it the absent cry of battered children
In the winter's cold restless and concerned
Who advance amidst the visors of vanished walls
Is it all this holding me fast in thrall to the image

Printed in
March 2004
at Gauvin Press Ltd., Hull, Québec